CATS IN A BASKET

By the same author

Bad Boys
Wagging Tales

Cats in a Basket

Edited by Eileen Colwell
Illustrated by Vanessa Julian-Ottie

VIKING

VIKING

Published by the Penguin Group
Penguin Books Ltd, 27 Wrights Lane, London W8 5TZ, England
Penguin Books USA Inc., 375 Hudson Street, New York, New York 10014, USA
Penguin Books Australia Ltd, Ringwood, Victoria, Australia
Penguin Books Canada Ltd, 10 Alcorn Avenue, Toronto, Ontario, Canada M4V 3B2
Penguin Books (NZ) Ltd, 182–190 Wairau Road, Auckland 10, New Zealand

Penguin Books Ltd, Registered Offices: Harmondsworth, Middlesex, England

First published 1993
10 9 8 7 6 5 4 3 2 1
First edition

This selection copyright © Eileen Colwell, 1993
Illustrations copyright © Vanessa Julian-Ottie, 1993

The Acknowledgements on pp. 122–3 constitute an extension of this copyright page

All rights reserved. Without limiting the rights under copyright reserved
above, no part of this publication may be reproduced, stored in or
introduced into a retrieval system, or transmitted, in any form or by any
means (electronic, mechanical, photocopying, recording or otherwise),
without the prior written permission of the copyright owner and the above
publisher of this book

Typeset by DatIX International Limited, Bungay, Suffolk
Filmset in 17/20 pt Monophoto Imprint
Printed in England by Clays Ltd, St Ives plc

A CIP catalogue record for this book is available from the British Library

ISBN 0–670–83710–5

Contents

The Box Under the Table
    RUTH AINSWORTH   7

Kitten
    VALERIE WORTH   15

The Invisible Kitten
    EILEEN COLWELL   17

Pompom and Pompinette
    PIXIE O'HARRIS   26

The Skitter-Skatter Cat
    ADRIENNE JONES   29

Cat Nonsense
    Riddle Cum Diddle, Diddle Cum Doodle
    LAURA RICHARDS   41
    There Once Were Two Cats in Kilkenny
    ANON   42

An Unusual Basket
    JILL TOMLINSON   43

Miss Tibbles
    IAN SERRAILLIER   58

Gobbolino's Hallowe'en
    URSULA MORAY WILLIAMS   60

The Owl and the Pussy-cat
    EDWARD LEAR   72

Two's Company
    HILARY DAVIES   75

Why the Manx Cat Has No Tail
    TRADITIONAL   88

Letting in the Light
    ELIZABETH LINDSAY   91

The Little White Cat
    Adapted by EILEEN COLWELL   93

Cat Nonsense
  Cats in Blue Jackets
    ANON   105
  My Uncle Paul of Pimlico
    MERVYN PEAKE   106

The Baker's Cat
    JOAN AIKEN   107

Cats
    ELEANOR FARJEON   120

Acknowledgements   122

The Box Under the Table

Two kittens lived with their mother in a box under the kitchen table. One was called Pansy because her face was like a black, crumpled pansy. She was a good little kitten. The other was called Tip because he had a white tip to his tail. He was a bad little kitten. Their mother, Minnie, loved them both and thought they were the best kittens in the world.

The kitchen belonged to a woman in a white apron called Mrs Plum.

She swept and dusted and poked the fire and rattled the pots and pans. Sometimes she filled a pail with soapy water and scrubbed the floor. When this happened, she lifted up the box with the kittens inside and put it on the kitchen table, so it should not get wet. Then the kittens had a good view of the whole kitchen. The dresser with the cups and saucers in neat rows. The clock on the mantelpiece. The shining brass door-handle. Everything.

'How big the world is,' said Tip, peeping over the edge of the box while Mrs Plum scrubbed the floor. 'One day I shall explore every corner. Will you come with me?'

'I don't know,' said little Pansy. 'I am afraid of the monster with red tongues who lives inside the kitchen stove and eats lumps of coal. He roars and crackles.'

'*I* am not afraid of him,' said Tip

bravely. 'I shall go right up to him and spit like this – P-t-t! P-t-t! Then *he* will be afraid of *me*. I shall growl, too, like this – G-r-r! G-r-r!'

That morning, after the floor was dry, Mrs Plum put some milk into a saucer and lifted the kittens out of the box and stood them on the floor, one each side of the saucer. 'You must learn to drink milk like your mother,' said Mrs Plum. 'Minnie! Minnie! Come and show your children how to lap milk.'

Minnie came out from the brush cupboard where she had been watching a mouse-hole and her green eyes shone when she saw the milk. She stretched her neck till her mouth was level with the saucer and her pink tongue flicked in and out, flick-flick-flick – and she lapped the milk. 'Now, my kittens, you try to lap,' she said. 'It is quite easy.'

Tip put his nose in too far and

sneezed, A-tish-oo! A-tish-oo! and spluttered milk over the clean floor, but Minnie quickly licked it up before Mrs Plum noticed. Pansy got on a little better. She curved her tiny tongue and tried to flick it in and out and lap up the milk.

'You are very slow,' said Minnie. 'Now I am going into the garden to sharpen my claws on the apple tree. When I come in I hope the saucer will be empty. One day when you can drink milk properly, I will take you into the garden and show you many wonderful things.'

Minnie padded softly out of the kitchen.

'I don't like this horrid cold milk,' said Tip. 'Do you?'

'Not very much,' sighed Pansy, 'and I am tired of trying to lap.'

'Let's paddle in the milk,' said naughty Tip and he stood right in the middle of the saucer. When he got out, each paw left a milky mark like a star on the floor. Pansy paddled next and then her paws left milky stars as well. They pattered all over the floor leaving milky prints everywhere.

Tip stopped by the coal-scuttle and looked inside. 'I shall try some of this coal,' he said. 'The fire-monster eats lots of it every day, so it should be nice.' He licked a black lump till his tongue was as black as the coal.

'Is it good?' asked Pansy.

'It tastes very odd,' said Tip, licking away. 'Perhaps I shall be able to crackle and roar when I have eaten enough.'

Just then they heard creak-creak-creak and thud-thud-thud. This was Mrs Plum coming downstairs. The kittens scampered across the floor and scrambled into their box.

'What a mess!' said Mrs Plum, looking at the milky footmarks. 'I'll give you what-for.'

The kittens did not know what 'what-for' meant, but it sounded like something horrid, so they shut their eyes and pretended to be asleep.

When Minnie came in from the garden she was shocked to see the mess her kittens had made.

'It is no good snoring,' she said crossly. 'I know you are only pretending to be asleep. Now wake up and let me wash you properly.' She started on Pansy and washed her from the tip of her pansy nose to the tip of her tail. Then came Tip's turn. He wriggled and squiggled and squeaked, but it was no good. Minnie held him firmly down with one paw and washed his ears and between his dusty little toes and everywhere.

'Tomorrow you must have another try with a saucer of milk,' said Minnie. 'Don't you want to grow into cats and climb trees and catch mice and sharpen your claws on the apple tree?'

'Yes, we do,' said Tip and Pansy.

'Mother, tell me what "what-for" is,' said Tip. 'Mrs Plum said she would give it to us if we were naughty.'

'Well,' said Minnie, 'it might be a smack or it might be a shake. Or it might be both. I hope you will never find out.'

The kittens hoped so too, and they made up their minds they would never be naughty again. (But I'm afraid they were!)

RUTH AINSWORTH

Kitten

The black kitten,
Arched stiff,
Dances side wise
From behind
The chair, leaps,
Tears away with
Ears back, spins,
Lands crouched
Flat on the floor,
Sighting something
At nose level,

Her eyes round
As oranges, her
Hind legs marking
Time: then she
Pounces, cactus-
Clawed, upon
A strayed
Strand of fluff:
Can anyone
Believe that she
Doesn't ask us
To laugh?

VALERIE WORTH

The Invisible Kitten

There once was a very unhappy kitten. The family with which it lived moved away and, by accident, left it behind. So a neighbour, Mrs Brown, had to take it in, but she didn't want a cat and didn't even *like* cats. She was always complaining that the kitten was in the way. One day, Mrs Brown even said, 'I wish that kitten would find itself another home so that I needn't see it again. Such a nuisance!'

The kitten was so upset that it became invisible, so that it couldn't be seen at all. (Its mother had once been a witch's cat, so it knew things like that.) Then it set off to find a new home. After all, no one wanted it and nobody had even bothered to give it a name. It *did* have a name it had chosen for itself, but that was a secret until it found a good home.

For several days the kitten wandered about looking for scraps of food. One day it discovered a puddle of milk on a doorstep where a bottle had overturned. It was delicious! Suddenly the housewife opened the door. To her surprise she saw a trail of milky pawmarks appearing down the *empty* path. 'How strange!' she said. 'I can't *see* a cat!'

The kitten became thinner and thinner. It did miaow for help but the thread of sound was so faint that no one noticed it.

One day it wandered into the park. A little girl was sitting on a seat with her mother, eating an ice-cream. A big blob fell on the seat and in a flash the kitten jumped up and began to lick it. The little girl, surprised, watched the ice-cream disappearing and put out her hand towards it. She touched warm, soft fur!

'Mummy,' she said, 'there's a pussy here!'

'Is there, Penny dear?' said her mother. Then, turning to another woman who was sitting beside her, she remarked, 'Wonderful what children can imagine, isn't it!'

'Mummy,' said Penny. 'Can I take this pussy home with me?'

'Oh, all right, dear,' her mother replied, for she thought that a 'pretend' kitten couldn't be much trouble, could it?

So Penny picked up the kitten

lovingly and tucked it inside her coat where it snuggled down and purred for the very first time in its life.

When they got home, Penny asked, 'Can I give Pussy some milk, Mummy?'

'Very well, dear,' said her mother, for she thought, 'It's not like feeding a real cat. A "pretend" cat can't eat much, can it?'

At bedtime Penny took the kitten with her, for although her mother didn't approve of animals in bed, she thought that a 'pretend' cat was different. So Penny and the kitten snuggled down happily together.

In the morning, Penny asked her mother if she might take the kitten with her to the play-group.

'I suppose so, dear,' said her mother. 'It's not as if it's a *real* cat . . .'

'But it is real!' protested Penny, hugging the kitten. Just for a second,

Penny's mother had a strange fancy that she *saw* a kitten in Penny's arms. How silly! She must be getting as fanciful as Penny. You couldn't possible *see* a 'pretend' kitten, could you?

At play-group, she warned the Leader that Penny had an imaginary kitten.

'Ah! Children!' agreed the Leader.

'I've got a kitten,' Penny said to her best friend, Joan. 'I'll let you stroke it.'

'Where is it?' asked Joan. 'I can't see one.'

'It's here!' protested Penny indignantly. 'Feel it!'

'There *is* a kitten!' agreed Joan. Soon the other children were crowding round trying to stroke the 'pretend' kitten. Before long they were nearly fighting for a turn.

'That's enough!' said the Leader crossly. 'Don't be silly. You can't stroke something that isn't there.'

'I saw its white paws,' said Joan.

'I seed its black tail!' shouted Fred. There was so much noise that the Leader was glad when play-group was over.

When Penny got home, her

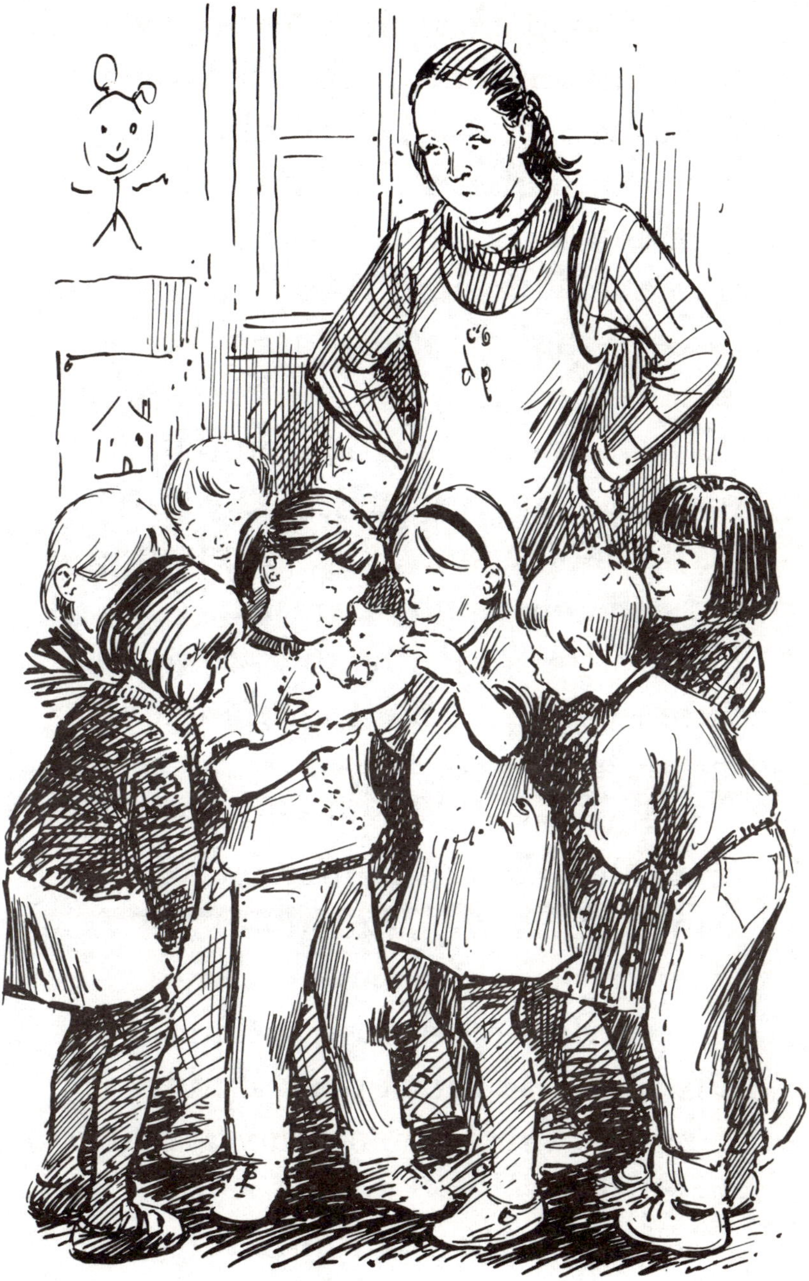

mother said, 'Darling, it's time you forgot about this "pretend" kitten. It's causing too much trouble. It's not as though it's a real kitten . . .'

'But it is real,' wailed Penny. 'I won't send it away!' She cried herself to sleep that night – it made the kitten's fur quite wet.

In the morning, you would have been able to see nearly all the kitten, if you had looked. It was beginning to be visible again because it so liked being stroked. Penny didn't notice because she had been seeing it a little more each day.

Penny carried the kitten downstairs but it jumped out of her arms and ran to her mother. 'Miaow!' it said, in its tiny voice.

Penny's mother turned and then – CRASH – she dropped a cup. 'There is a real kitten!' she gasped. 'I can see it!'

'I told you so – you are funny,

Mummy,' said Penny. 'Its name is Twinkle,' and she hugged the kitten until it purred with pleasure.

Then the kitten knew that it had found its proper home at last, for Penny had called it by its secret name, which nobody knew except the kitten itself.

And, do you know, Twinkle never had to be invisible again, for he was so happy to be wanted.

EILEEN COLWELL

Pompom and Pompinette

Who could ever quite forget
The twins Pompom and Pompinette
Neglected by a flighty mother.
They turned for comfort to each
   other.

They wandered and they found a
   friend
Down Bay Street, just around the
   bend,
And there they grew up unafraid
Until one sad day Pompom strayed.

Such lonely days for Pompinette,
She worked herself into a fret.
She searched for Pompom in the
   cave,
Around the rocks and in the wave.

And then – what everyone had
   feared –
Pompinette also disappeared . . .

One night, the moon was riding high,
I'm sure I saw them passing by,

Miaowing words both strange and kind,
Two kittens with their tails entwined.

A little sister, little brother,
Each seemed whiter than the other
And each seemed well to know the way,
Along the moonpath through the spray.

The moon shone on them brightly yet,
I looked again – no Pompinette,
No Pompom either – vanished quite;
Two little ghost cats in the night.

PIXIE O'HARRIS

The Skitter-Scatter Cat
A story from America

I

Gramma and I took our usual walk last night. The sun was just setting, all red and gold, beyond the ocean. Night's shadow crept across the hills. Gram lives on a small island of houses with open land all around. The hills are covered with grass, green in the winter when it rains, golden in summer's hot sun. There are scattered clumps of sagebrush and a few thistles and tumbleweeds.

I love visiting Gram. We watch the

redtail hawks making high handsome turns in the sky. We see rabbits and possums and skunks and ground squirrels. Once a racoon. Once a weasel. Sometimes we even find a big furry tarantula spider whose looks are worse than its bite. Gram even lets the tarantula walk on her hand.

'Eight-legged cats,' she tells me, laughing. We like to joke.

Gram and I love cats.

At night we can hear coyotes in the hills. Gram says they're singing. Really they are howling and yipping at each other through the dark. Maybe they're lonesome. Or maybe they are hunting. People with cats and small dogs keep them safe indoors at night.

Last evening, two streets from Gram's place, we passed a darkened two-storey house. Another street and we'd have been out in the hills. Something came bounding out of the shadows at the side of the house. A small something, but it made us jump.

'Such a skitter-scatter little cat!' Gram exclaimed.

'With golden eyes like a lion's,' I said.

'Yes.' And we laughed together at the antics of the kitten.

His soft grey coat blended with the evening shadows. But even in the gloom his white feet were easy to see, and the last of the light touched his pink nose and brightened the white triangle under his chin. But skitter-scatter he was. He bounded away before us. He circled back and leaped and pounced and sun-fished and crouched and sprang and scurried and hid and burst out at us again. He followed us as we walked to the farthest edge of houses.

'We can't go out in the hills this evening,' I said.

'No. We can't,' Gram agreed. 'Our

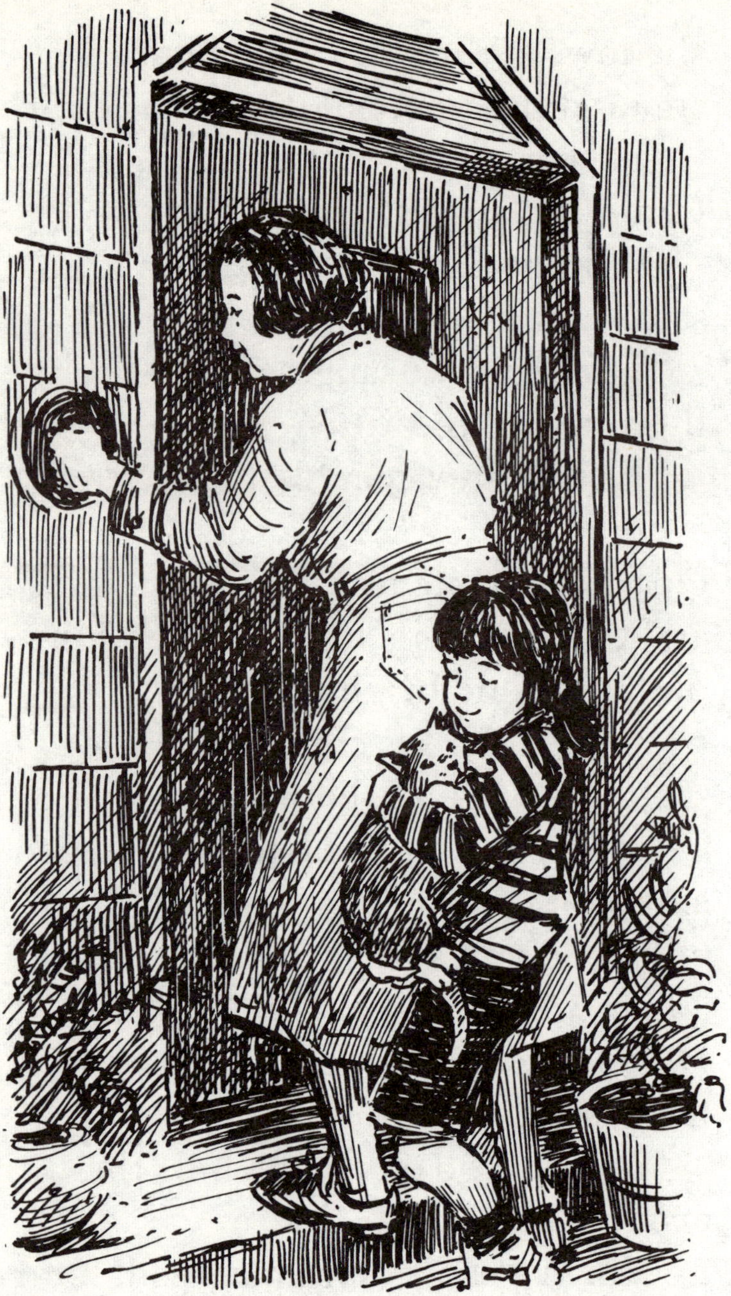

furry friend might skitter away into the sagebrush. He might get lost in the tall grass.'

'His family would never find him.'

'And there are the coyotes.'

'The two-storey house must be his. Let's go back and ring the bell,' I said.

'He might be a stray.' Gram bent to touch his soft grey coat.

The kitten did a nip-up and dodged her touch. Then as though apologizing, he came back and rubbed against her leg.

'Wouldn't you like to carry him, Jeannie?' She picked him up and handed him to me. 'We'll go back and ring the bell.'

He nestled in my arms all the way to the dark house. Gram rang the bell once. We could hear its chime behind the front door. She waited a minute, then she rang again. And, finally, again.

'No one's home,' she decided. 'Let's ask up and down the street. Maybe someone knows where the kitten lives.'

The man at the first house said, 'He's not our cat,' and shut the door.

'I've never seen him before,' said the little girl at the next house. 'But if he's lost maybe he can live with me.' She turned and spoke to someone out of sight. 'May I have a kitty, Papa?'

We could only hear a voice. 'No,' it said.

By the time we tried the fifth house the skitter-scatter kitten was restless in my arms. He struggled and mewed, and put up a terrible fuss.

'Let's try the two-storey again,' Gram said.

But by the time we stood before the darkened house, the little cat was frantic. He squirmed from my arms, hit the ground running, bounced and skittered around the corner of the house and was gone.

We finished our walk alone. Finally, back at Gram's house, we read some stories together. When I crawled into bed in the guest room, I was already sleepy. As I drifted off there was the little skitter-scatter cat in my dreams. He was hiding beneath a thistle bush. His golden eyes were as large as moons. He stared out at a circle of foxy coyote faces, at their raised lips and sharp teeth.

I awoke a long time later. The moon shone in my window. The coyotes were singing. They were very close. It sounded as though they were in the park below Gram's house. They had set up a great caterwauling, yipping and howling. Then suddenly they stopped. The silence was as cold and silver as the moonlight.

I shivered. Had they caught a

small grey cat with white feet and a white triangle beneath his chin?

Next evening on our walk, Gram and I watched for our four-legged friend. The two-storey house was still dark. No skitter-scatter cat came bounding out. Nor the next evening. Nor the next.

'The wicked coyotes must have gotten him.' I could feel my chin tremble.

Gram put her arm around me. 'Coyotes must live, too,' she told me. 'They're not really wicked, Jeannie. We took part of their hills when these houses were built. They catch whatever they can. A rabbit or a cat, it's all the same to them. Chances are that our bouncy friend is alive and well, though.' And Gram gave me a smile, trying to keep me from being sad.

2

It was some time before I could visit Gramma again. We went for our usual evening walks. The first night I tried not to watch for our kitten. The second, we walked a little faster past the two-storey house.

The third night we walked late. It was dark when Gram suddenly stopped. She pointed. There from beside the two-storey house came a sedate grey cat. His white-booted feet paced along with soft and delicate tread. His triangle beneath his chin seemed to glow. He held his elegant tail straight up. His golden eyes caught, reflected the street light.

'Miaow-w.' His gravelly voice creased the night.

I stooped, scratched beneath his ear. His pink nose touched my hand. His tongue was warm and rough on my arm. He turned and gave a fond rub to Gram's leg.

The door of the two-storey house opened. A boy stood there.

'Hey, Mungojerrie, don't you wander away!' The boy gave us a merry smile. 'He did once, you know.'

'Mungojerrie? What a funny name,' I said.

'We got it from a poem. Mungojerrie was a wicked cat. This one was full of the old nick when he was little.' The boy laughed, scooped up Mungojerrie, and disappeared inside the two-storey house.

'Our skitter-scatter kitten didn't make a coyote dinner after all.' I felt happy all over.

Gram sounded almost sad when she said, 'But he's all grown up.' She stood looking down at me. After a moment she smiled. 'He would probably have given the coyotes indigestion, anyway.'

Then we were laughing together.

'Let's go home, Jeannie.' Gram took my hand. 'I have a book with that poem in it, the one that mentions Mungojerrie. *Old Possum's Book of Practical Cats*. We'll read it together before you go to sleep tonight.'

ADRIENNE JONES

Cat Nonsense

Riddle cum diddle, diddle cum
   doodle,
My little cat's name is Toodle;
   I curled up her hair,
      But she only said, 'There!
You have made me look just like a
   poodle.'

                LAURA RICHARDS

There were once two cats in
   Kilkenny,
Each thought there was one cat too
   many
So they fought and they fit,
And they scratched and they bit,
Till, excepting their nails,
And the tip of their tails,
Instead of two cats, there weren't
   any.

ANON

An Unusual Basket

Suzy was a little striped cat. She had stiffly starched white whiskers and a fine pair of football socks on her front paws.

Suzy lived in the house of a fisherman in a little seaside village in France. The fisherman had four sons. Pierre was ten years old, Henri was eight, Paul was six and Gaby was four, so when they stood in a row they looked like a set of steps. All the boys played with Suzy and they took her with them everywhere.

Pierre, the eldest one, made Suzy a scratching-post by wrapping a bit of old carpet round one of the fat legs of the big kitchen table. Suzy could sharpen her claws whenever she liked.

Henri knew which were the best tickly places on her spotted tummy. Although all the rest of her was covered with black stripes, Suzy's tummy was fawn with black spots. Henri said she was a tiger on top and a leopard underneath. Anyway, he was a jolly good tickler.

Paul made a toy for her. He tied a piece of crackly paper to the end of a long piece of string and pulled it along on the ground for her to chase. Suzy could run very fast and Paul could not keep ahead of her for very long. She would pounce and catch the paper again and again. Paul would stand still to get his breath back and dangle the bit of paper just out of reach above her head. Suzy would leap and leap to catch it, with Paul jerking it away when she got too near. Paul was great fun.

But Gaby, the youngest, was the best. Suzy adored him – and for a very odd reason. Gaby didn't know the proper way to stroke a cat. Most cats like being stroked from head to tail, the way the fur lies. But Gaby always stroked Suzy the wrong way – backwards from tail to head – and Suzy *loved* it. She would wriggle against his hand with delight, purring like a sewing machine, asking him to do it again and again. She liked it better than anything else in the world. Yes, even better than eating fish. And Suzy liked eating fish very much indeed – which was just as well because she had it for breakfast and supper every day.

The boys always helped their father

when he came home in his boat with the catch of fish. Every day they waited for him on the quay – Pierre and Henri and Paul and Gaby and Suzy. She was allowed to eat as much as she liked of the fish that were too small to be sold. There was always something for Suzy even when the catch wasn't very good. She would have grown fat if the boys had not given her so much exercise.

Suzy hated it when the boys were at school and there was nobody to play with her; nobody to dangle a bit of string or throw a ball or climb trees with her. She would wander round the quay by herself getting in everybody's way, or go exploring in the fields behind the village.

One day she was chasing butterflies across a field when she nearly bumped into a huge basket. Suzy was used to baskets – there were lots of them on the quay – but this one was much bigger. Suzy

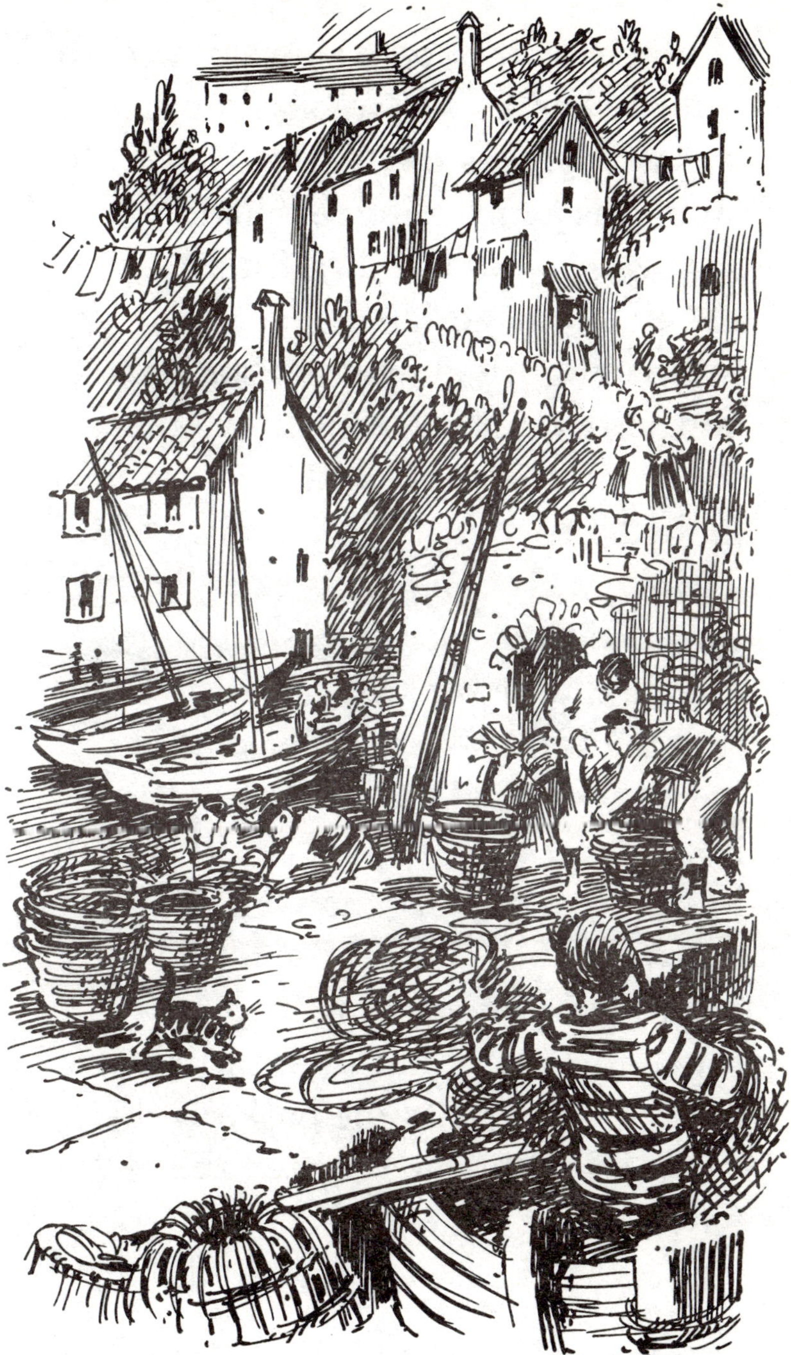

climbed up the steep side and peered in. The basket was so big that there was a wooden stool inside. Under the stool was a nice patch of shade.

It was a very hot day. Suzy decided to have a little nap. She jumped lightly down into the basket and settled herself nose to tail under the stool. Curled round like that she looked like a huge furry snail.

Suzy was soon fast asleep.

When she woke up Suzy felt most peculiar. The basket seemed to be rocking from side to side, joggling her. She rushed to the edge of the basket and climbed up the side to jump out – but she changed her mind when she looked over the top! The ground was a very long way away – much too far for her to jump. She clung on tightly as the basket jerked again, grabbing at a rope with her paws.

Ropes? She had not noticed them

when she climbed in. Suzy looked up. The ropes were attached to a huge balloon – an ENORMOUS balloon. Suzy was floating high up in the sky in a basket suspended from a balloon!

Poor Suzy! She slid back into the basket and crouched on the floor shivering with fright.

Then she felt a gentle hand on her back and looked up to find there was a man in the basket with her.

'Hello, little cat,' he said. 'I didn't invite you! Oh well, it's too late now. You will have to come with me to England.'

Suzy didn't know where England was, but she knew she didn't want to go there. She wanted to stay in France in her own little fishing village with the boys.

'Chez-moi!' she wailed. It sounded like 'shay-mwa'. She was saying in French that she wanted to go home.

But the man had to jump up to do something with the balloon, which was swinging wildly, and from then on was too busy to take any notice of his little passenger.

So Suzy floated across the sea

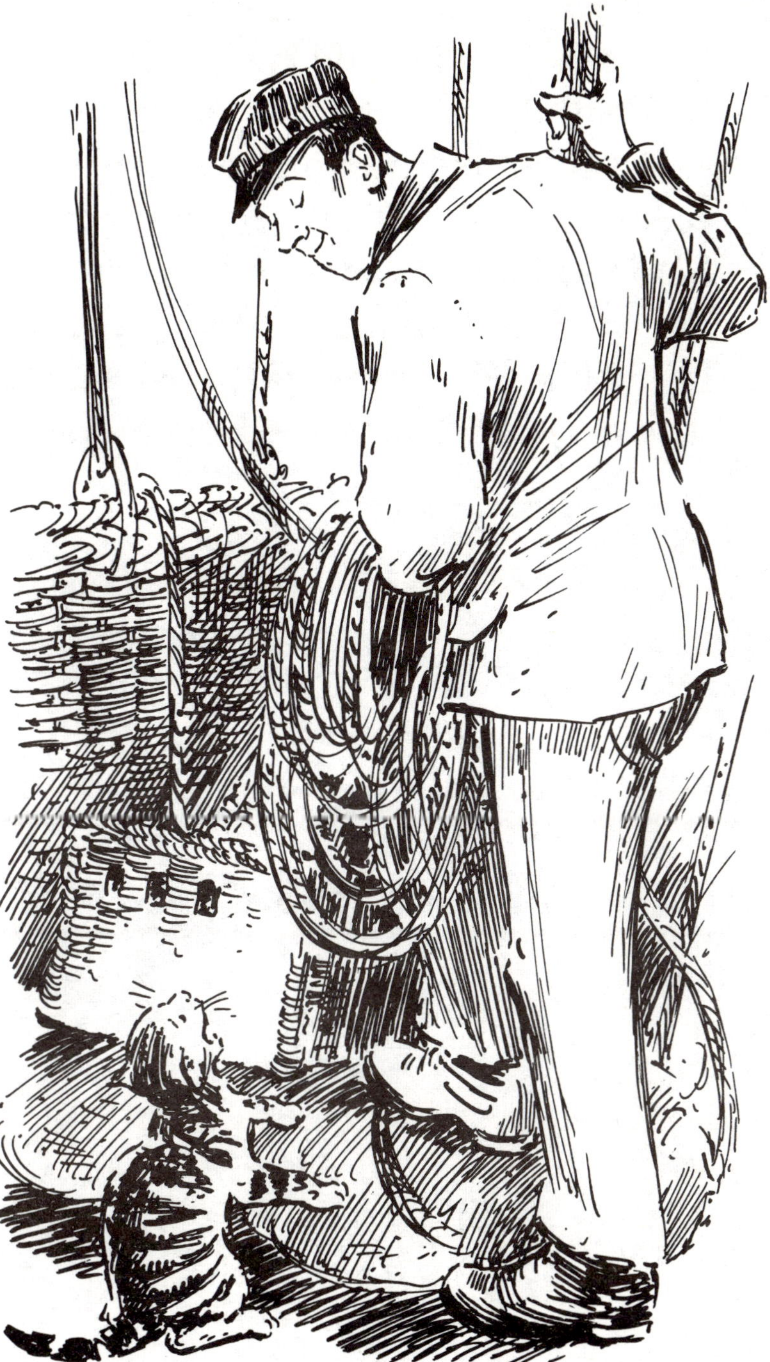

between France and England by balloon! She hated every joggly moment of it. The worst part was seeing the coast of France disappear behind them – France and Pierre and Henri, Paul and Gaby, France and everything she knew and loved.

'Chez-moi!' she wailed again, but

nobody heard her. There were big puffy clouds sailing underneath them and sometimes what looked like toy ships on the sea far below. It was really very interesting and beautiful but Suzy could only think about one thing. How was she going to get back across this huge stretch of water?

They landed in England with a bump. Suzy had not realized that they were back over land again because for the last bit she had had her eyes tightly shut. She jumped out of the basket and ran. She could not get away from that balloon fast enough.

Because she was very hungry, she ran towards a fishy smell. But the smell was coming from the sea and there were no fish and no fishing boats. This was an English seaside town and not a bit like her own village. There was just a wide expanse of concrete in front of the sea, with steps down to the sand. Poor Suzy. She sat miserably on the sea-front looking out at the waves. How was she going to get home across all that water?

Luckily an RSPCA lady came along. It was her job to find homes for lost cats. She picked up Suzy and

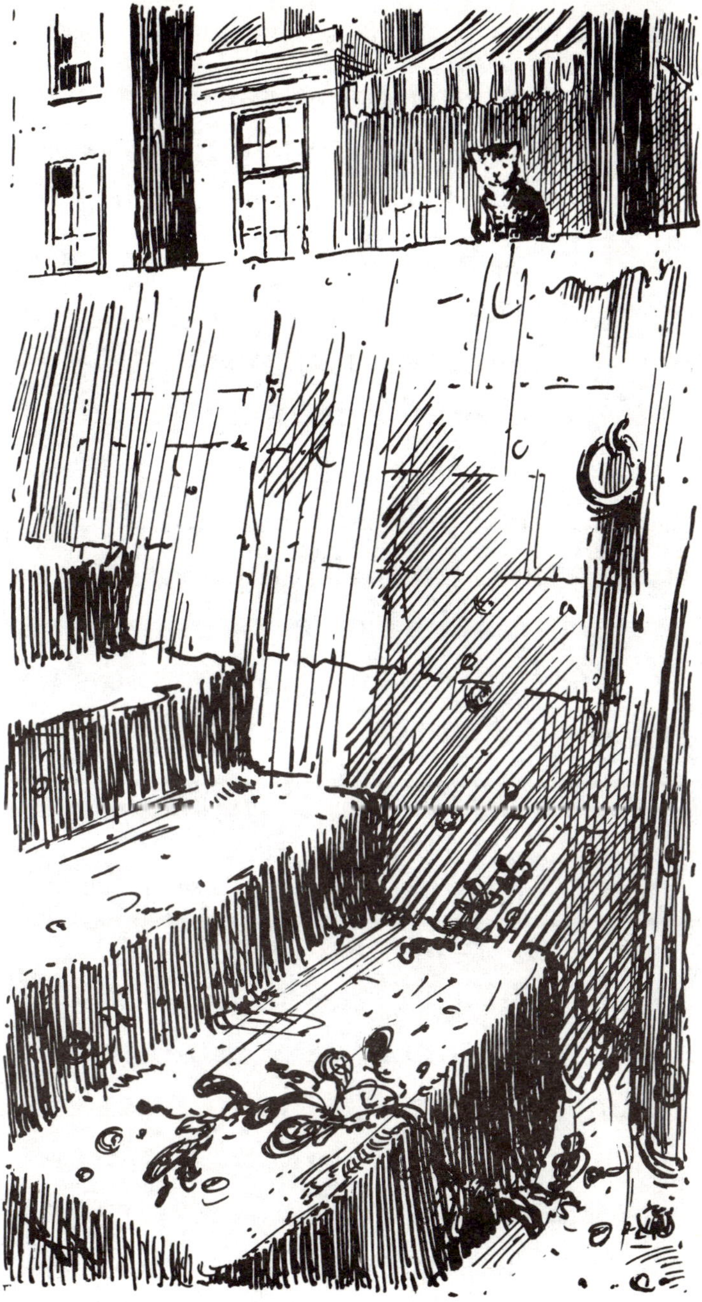

took her to the house of a kind old lady whom she knew, called Auntie Jo. 'Do you think you could look after this little cat for me, Auntie Jo?' the RSPCA lady said. 'I've never seen her before. She's not from around here. She must be lost.'

'Of course, she can stay with me,' said Auntie Jo.

Of course, Suzy could not understand English, but she understood the saucer of milk that Auntie Jo put down for her and she lapped up every drop. Then, because she was a polite cat, she said 'thank you' in French: 'Merci!' It was a miaowing sound, 'mare-see'.

'What a funny miaow you have, pussy-cat,' said Auntie Jo.

Suzy was made very comfortable on an old chair that night. Auntie Jo stroked her gently and Suzy purred. She purred in French, but purring sounds the same all over the world,

whatever country you come from.
 But it wasn't like home. She did miss Gaby stroking her the wrong way.

JILL TOMLINSON

(Suzy did get back to France, after many adventures.)

Miss Tibbles

Miss Tibbles is my kitten; white
As day she is and black as night.

She moves in little gusts and breezes
Sharp and sudden as a sneeze is.

At hunting Tibbles has no match,
How I like to see her catch

Moth or beetle, two a penny,
And feast until there isn't any!

Or, if they 'scape her, see her eyes
Grow big as saucers with surprise.

Sometimes I like her calm, unwild,
Gentle as a sleeping child,

And wonder as she lies, a fur ring,
Curled upon my lap, unstirring –
Is it me or Tibbles purring?

                IAN SERRAILLIER

Gobbolino's Hallowe'en

Gobbolino, the Witch's cat, had found a home at last with a kind farmer and his wife and their friendly children. Gobbolino had always wanted to be a kitchen cat.

There was only one animal on the farm who was not his friend and that was Noggins, the old black horse who was the farmer's pride and joy. Noggins did half the work on the farm, and the farmer often said that he could not manage without him. But Noggins took no notice at all of Gobbolino, which was very unfortunate, for they had to share the stable at night.

Summer passed by, with hay-time and harvest, and then it was Hallowe'en. The big black horse had been restless all day long, but, much to Gobbolino's surprise, he began a conversation when the farmer shut them into the stable at night.

'Little Gobbolino! Do you know what day it is?'

'Oh yes, I do, I do! It is Hallowe'en, the night when witches are about,' said Gobbolino, happy to be safely indoors on such an evening.

'Gobbolino! Are the stars shining? Is the moon full?' asked Noggins.

'Yes, the moon is full and the stars are shining!'

'Open the stable door so that I can see the moon and the stars!' said the black horse.

Gobbolino did not dare to open the full stable door in case Noggins should get out, but he opened the top half with his paw. The black horse whinnied with excitement.

'Gobbolino! Do you know who I really am?' said Noggins.

'No!' said Gobbolino, frightened by the big horse's flashing eyes and stamping hoofs.

'Jump on my back and I will show you!' said the black horse mysteriously.

Gobbolino did not want to jump on his back, but he was afraid of offending him so he did as he was told. At once the horse gave a whinny that sounded like the howl of the wind.

'I am . . . I am . . . A WITCH'S BROOMSTICK!' it cried fiercely, and cleared the half-door of the stable door with a bound. To his terror, Gobbolino realized that the

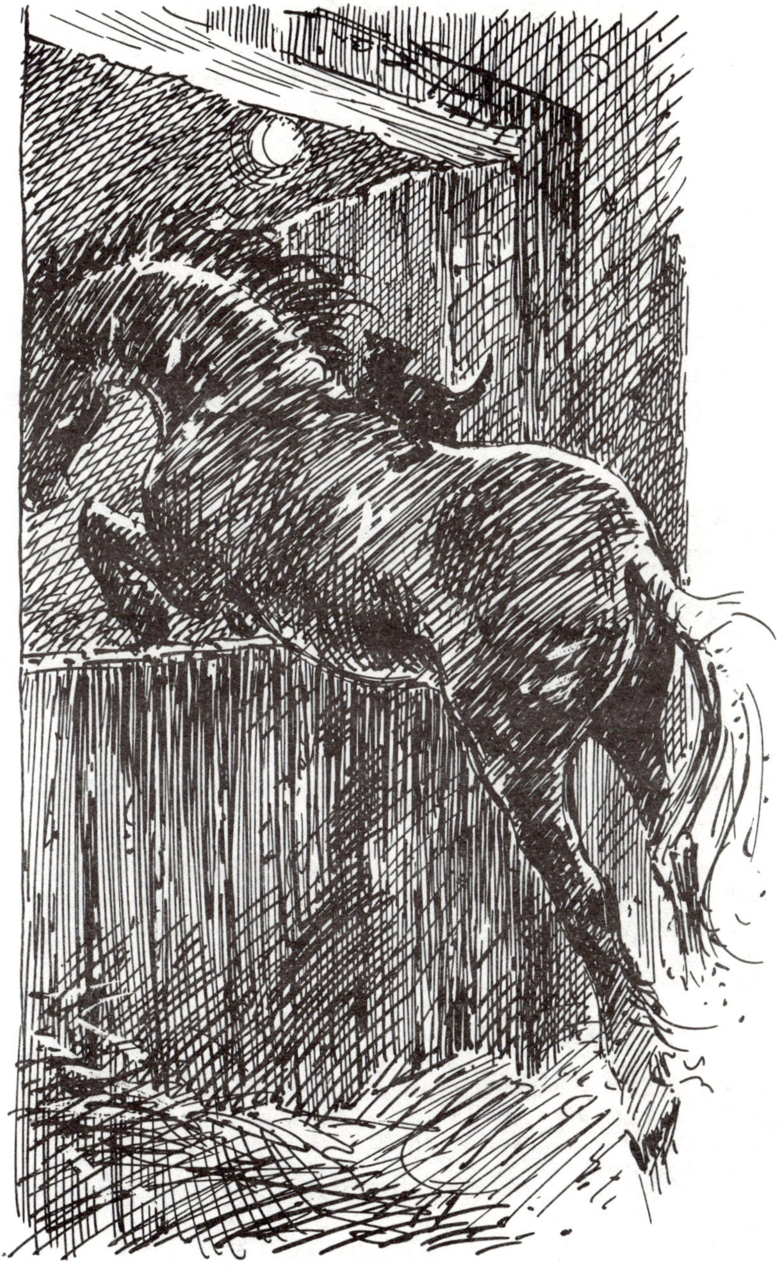

horse's broad, warm back had become a hard wooden broomstick!

Out, out sprang the broomstick into the night sky, with Gobbolino clinging desperately to the shaft and begging piteously to return.

'What will the master do without you?' wailed Gobbolino. 'He has been good and kind to you all your life. How can you treat him so? Oh, why couldn't you leave me at home – all I want is to be a kitchen cat!'

'Never fear, little Gobbolino!' sang the broomstick. 'By sunrise I shall be a horse again! When Hallowe'en is over I must be back in my stable or else I'll be a broomstick for ever and ever. Let's have fun, Gobbolino! Let's enjoy ourselves while Hallowe'en lasts! You have been a witch's cat, so you know what sport it is to ride the skies on Hallowe'en!'

At these words Gobbolino's heart throbbed with relief and he began to actually enjoy the ride. It was a long time since he had ridden on a broomstick, and the last time he had been terribly frightened. Now he joined in the horse's wild delight and miaowed with excitement as they swooped between the stars.

All of a sudden, he called out in alarm: 'Noggins! Noggins! I can hear voices behind us! I can see broomsticks! We are being chased by witches!'

It was quite true. Gaining on them fast were half a dozen hideous witches, crying out: 'A broomstick! A runaway broomstick! And a cat! We'll have them! Catch them! Catch them!'

The broomstick doubled its speed. Gobbolino lay crouched on the shaft, his ears pressed close to his head. They flew across the valley at a tremendous speed and up the sides of the Hurricane Mountain, with the

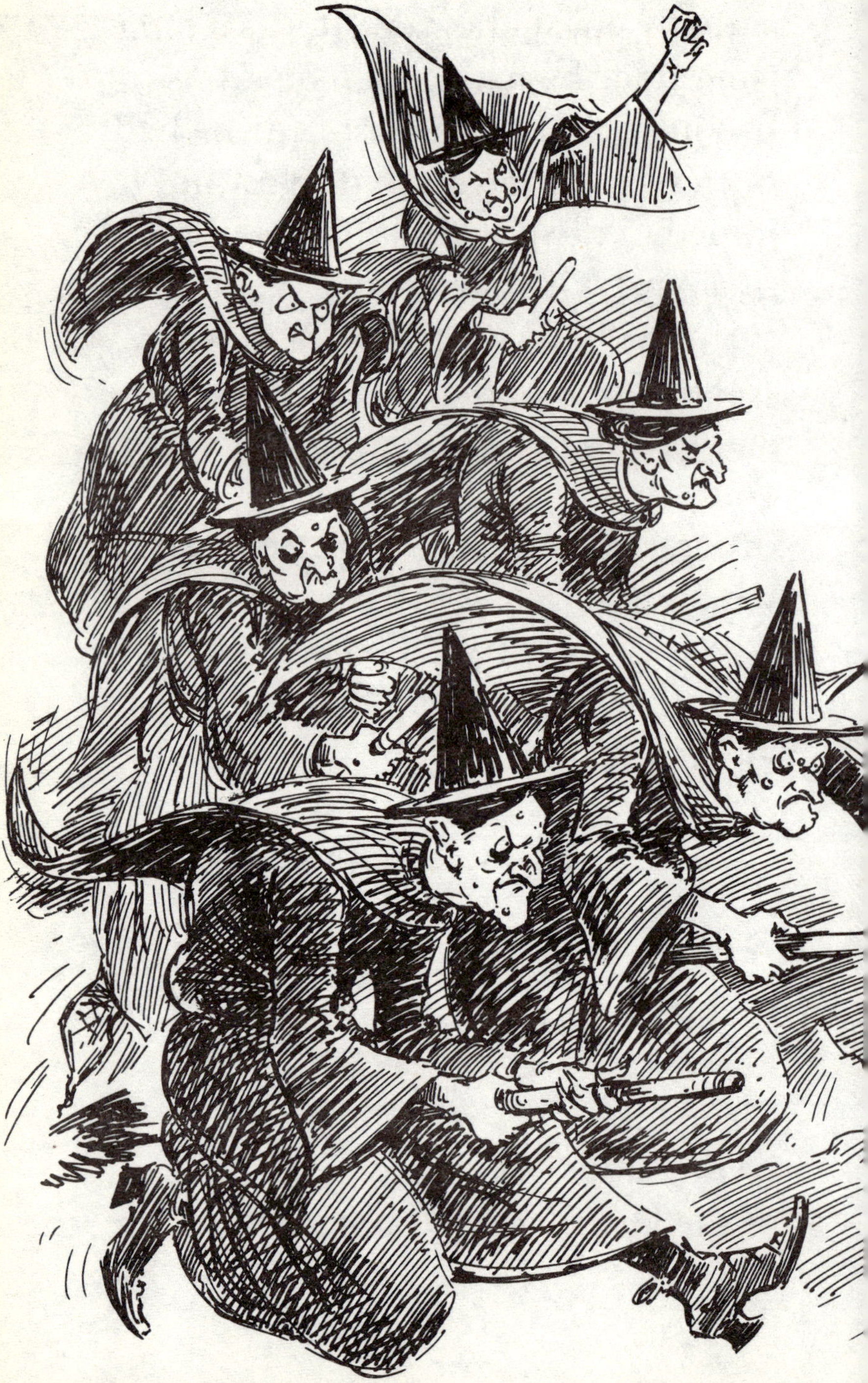

witches shrieking close on their heels. Half-way up the peaks there was a goatherd's shed, and into this the broomstick hurled itself, hoping to escape from the flying witches behind them.

But the witches had seen his trick and the next moment they were all at the door, looking inside and pointing with their long, skinny fingers as they jeered in chorus: 'That's no broomstick! That's old Noggins from the farm! And that's no witch's cat!

It's just a common little pussycat! Come away, sisters! Shut the door on them and come up over the mountains! Hallowe'en will soon be over!'

The door slammed shut. The witches disappeared in a chorus of screeches. Although Gobbolino scratched and the broomstick kicked, they could not open it.

Hour after hour went by and the witches did not return.

'I am finished,' said the broomstick in despair. 'I shall never get home before sunrise! And what use shall I be to the master if I stay a broomstick all my life?'

Gobbolino lifted up his voice in a despairing miaow, so loud that it was carried by the wind to the top of the mountain. It was heard by the little mice that had known him as a kitten in the witch's cave where he had been born. He had always been kind to the mice and had not teased them as his sister Sootica had done.

'That is Gobbolino, the witch's cat! He is in trouble!' said the mice. 'We must go and help him!'

Down the mountain pattered dozens of little feet as, one behind the other, the mice hurried along the path to the goatherd's shed. Gobbolino saw them coming through a chink in the door.

'Oh, little mice! Little mice!' he cried joyfully. 'Please make a hole in the door for us, so my friend the broomstick and I can escape from this hut! The witches have shut us up inside, and we *must* get home before the sun rises!'

There was a pale glow now in the eastern sky. The sun would soon be rising over the top of the mountain.

The mice set to work with a will, squeaking with excitement. Soon the grinding and snapping of hundreds of teeth made the splinters fly, and a round hole appeared in the door. Gobbolino squeezed himself through in a minute, but it took quite an effort for the broomstick to force its bristles through the small space, and now the sky was the colour of ripe apricots. There was no time to be lost!

Crying their thanks to the mice, Gobbolino and the broomstick raced across the sky for home. The valley slipped away beneath them. The long blue dawn-shadows of the mountains reached out their fingers to touch them and then fled away backwards as the sun rose.

The first beams chased them into the farmyard just as Noggins, the black horse, panting for breath, clattered across the cobblestones on ironshod feet.

'Why, however did Noggins get out?' the farmer cried in surprise, looking out of his bedroom window.

'And there is little Gobbolino riding on his back for all the world as if he had brought him home again! I never thought those two had much to say to each other!'

But now they had a secret to share, Gobbolino and Noggins were friends for ever and ever.

URSULA MORAY WILLIAMS

The Owl and the Pussy-cat

The Owl and the Pussy-Cat went to
   sea
   In a beautiful pea-green boat,
They took some honey, and plenty
   of money,
   Wrapped up in a five-pound note.
The Owl looked up to the stars
   above,
   And sang to a small guitar,
'O lovely Pussy! O Pussy, my love,
   What a beautiful Pussy you are,
      You are,
      You are!
What a beautiful Pussy you are!'

Pussy said to the Owl, 'You elegant fowl!
　　How charmingly sweet you sing!
O let us be married! too long have we tarried:
　　But what shall we do for a ring?'
They sailed away for a year and a day,
　　To the land where the Bong-tree grows,
And there in a wood a Piggy-wig stood,
　　With a ring at the end of his nose,
　　　　His nose,
　　　　His nose,
With a ring at the end of his nose.

'Dear Pig, are you willing to sell for one shilling
   Your ring?' Said the Piggy, 'I will.'
So they took it away, and were married next day
   By the Turkey who lives on the hill.
They dined on mince, and slices of quince,
   Which they ate with a runcible spoon:
And hand in hand, on the edge of the sand,
They danced by the light of the moon,
      The moon,
      The moon,
They danced by the light of the moon.

EDWARD LEAR

Two's Company

Sparky's ears pricked up. Yes, the sound of footsteps was approaching the kitchen door. It would be Master coming down into the kitchen, as he did every morning, to let Sparky out into the garden. Then he would open the blind and put on the kettle.

Sparky was a black cat and he'd got his name because his Master said 'he seemed a bright young spark', the liveliest of a litter of kittens looking for a home. He'd been living with this family now for five years and was very happy.

Sparky yawned and stepped out of his basket, then ran obediently to the kitchen door. 'Good little cat,' said his Master with a rough caress to his black fur, and Sparky gently licked his hand before shooting off into the garden.

Just as he thought. No one else about. All the birds, lazy things, must be still asleep. He noticed they never came to the bird table until later, for they knew well when their food would be put out. He wondered where they slept? The big tree with its bare branches had no birds perched on it.

After a brisk run round the garden to get warm, and then a nibble of grass, Sparky leapt on to the kitchen step, eyes bright, waiting for the door to open. He knew his breakfast would be waiting – clean, new milk and

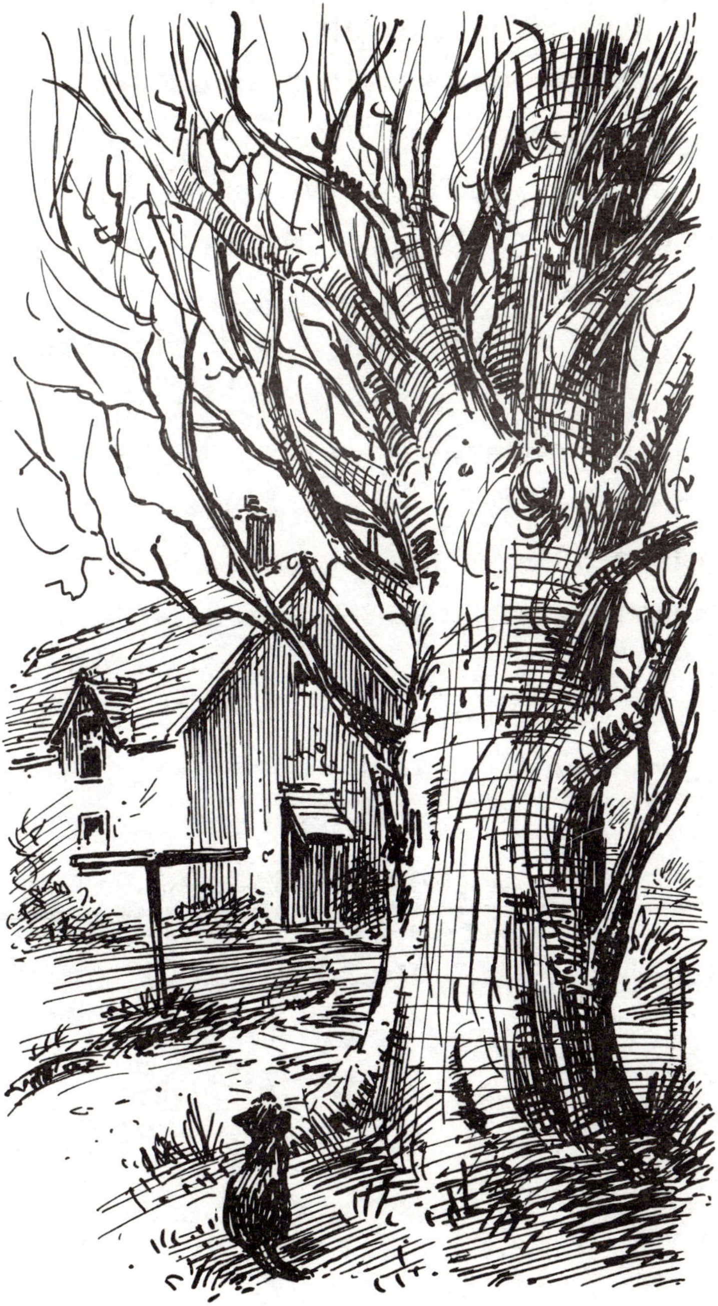

some tasty meat – but he was longing to get inside to see his friend more than to eat.

Strange, the door remained shut. Where were they all? No good giving a 'miaow', for his voice was small after a dose of 'flu he'd had. Standing on his hind legs, he rattled the door knob vigorously – and the door was opened so suddenly that he almost fell into the warm kitchen. Hastily resuming an upright position, Sparky checked to see that his food was in its accustomed place. Then, disdainfully ignoring the saucers, he sped into the front room and leapt to the top of the sofa, scattering garden earth as he went. Mistress wouldn't be very pleased. He started to clean his paws, but as he did so he peeped several times at his friend's cage.

Feathers, the parrot, his friend, was still covered over and obviously asleep. Sparky wondered what they would do today? Even if Feathers only talked about his adventures on the pirate ship, it would be exciting.

Sparky chased his tail absent-mindedly. Mistress came into the room and scolded him about the grit on her sofa. 'Good morning, Feathers,' she said, taking off the brown cover from the cage. Feathers, a brilliant green and red bird, opened one eye and closed it again. Sparky chased round the chairs and rubbed himself against his mistress's leg.

'I haven't time to play today,' she said. 'I have to go out and I hope you will both be good!' She gave Feathers his fresh seed and water and went out of the room.

Feathers was very old, about a hundred years old, Sparky thought. He had been here when Sparky had first arrived. Sparky ran into the kitchen and quickly drank up his milk. Then he rushed back into the

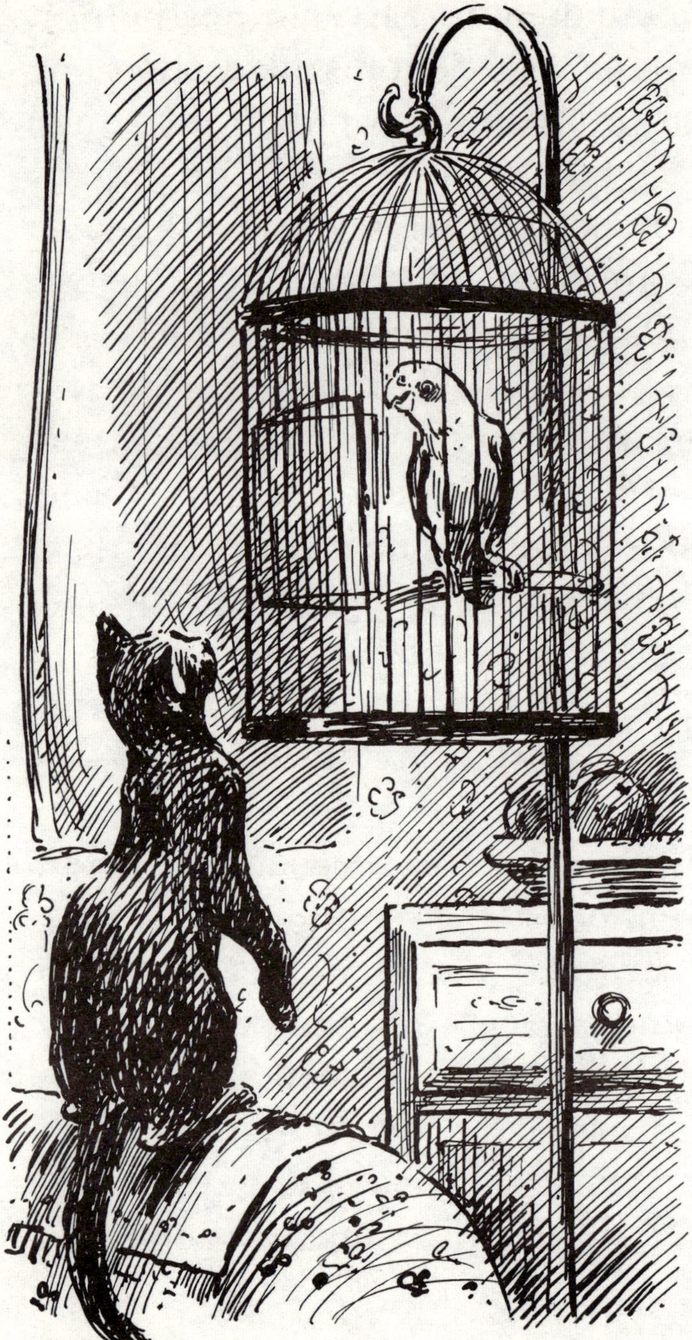

front room. Feathers was preening himself. 'Good morrow, me Hearty,' he said as he fluffed out his tail feathers.

'Oh, Feathers, what shall we do today?' asked Sparky. 'It's cold, but the sun is shining and it would be nice if we could do something exciting!'

Feathers pecked at his seed. Then he cackled, 'Look at the door! Look at the door!'

Sparky looked but it seemed no different from when he'd come in. Feathers squawked crossly, 'The *cage* door, silly!' Then Sparky noticed that the little hook which generally held the cage door shut wasn't fastened at all. What a bit of good luck, but how could Feathers open it? It would be terribly difficult.

'Watch me!' cackled Feathers. He crouched on his perch, then he *flung* himself at the door. It burst open with a crash and Feathers tumbled out.

How glorious to be free! He stretched out his wings and flew round and round the room while Sparky chased round after him admiringly. What a wonderful day this was!

'Let's go outside,' suggested Sparky – but then he hesitated. Wouldn't it be too cold for a rare bird, used only to hot climates, to venture out into an English garden? Then he had an idea. The nearby Conservatory was warm and housed lots of tropical plants. Surely Feathers would be glad to see some of his favourite native plants again?

The Conservatory wasn't far away. It was in the park, which was very near to their house. The garden fence bordered the park and although people had to walk right round by two roads to reach it, animals could make a short cut. 'Come on, Feathers,' said Sparky. 'I know where we can go.' He darted into the kitchen and Feathers followed.

It was a bit difficult for Feathers to get through the cat-flap, but he managed it and swooped over the garden before soaring over the fence, while Sparky scrambled underneath it.

They were lucky. The door of the Conservatory was open and a gardener was removing some tools. The friends darted in and hid behind a large green plant. The gardener finished his task and went out again.

What now? Sparky's heart was beating fast. Feathers was swinging from the thick twisted branch of a tropical tree and making clicking noises of pleasure with his beak. There were brilliant flowers everywhere and a little stream ran down one side of the big glass house.

It was warm and steamy, like being in a jungle.

'This reminds me of home,' cackled Feathers. 'What a lovely place! I wish I could stay for ever.'

Sparky put a paw into the little stream. There were no fish but he could see an interesting face looking back. He bent closer to look – and fell in! It was his own reflection!

Wet through and shivering, he scrambled out, and shook himself. The drops of water flew off his fur and sparkled like a rainbow. He soon dried, luckily. It was so warm.

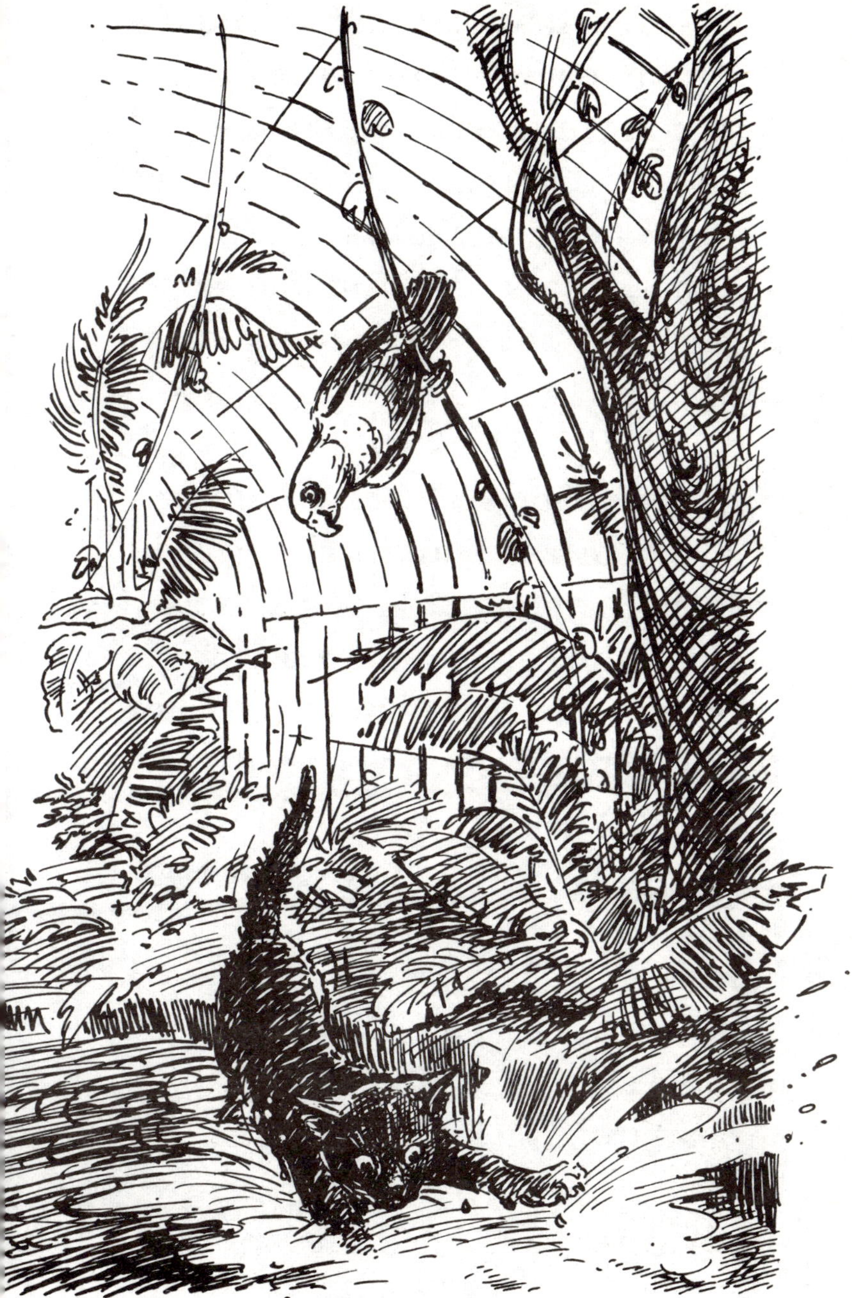

Feathers flew carefully round, stopping to admire the orchids and coloured fruits. He found a nut and cracked it open with his beak. It was a long time since he had tasted nuts like that! Sparky had found a ball of string and was having a fine game with it.

Suddenly a clock struck three and the door opened. Hearts beating faster, Feathers and Sparky crouched, hidden, as the gardener came inside again with a barrow!

Sparky darted out and Feathers swooped to the open door. Startled at seeing a bright, beautiful bird flash past him, the gardener overbalanced and tipped out the contents of his barrow!

Safely home, Feathers flew quickly into his cage again and Sparky slipped into the kitchen to drink up his milk.

Mistress came back a few minutes

later. 'Oh, my goodness! I left the cage open. What luck Feathers didn't fly away!' she said.

She didn't see Feathers and Sparky wink at each other . . .

HILARY DAVIES

Why the Manx Cat Has No Tail

A story from the Isle of Man

In the old days when Noah was filling the Ark with two of every animal, one of the cats went out mousing. She took a notion that she wouldn't go into the Ark without a mouse inside her, for well she knew that once she was there not a one would she be allowed to taste.

All the other animals were safe inside the Ark and already the rain had begun to fall. There was still no sign of the cat, so Noah said, 'Well, that's that. There'll be no she-cat!'

He was just closing the door when the cat came up, half-drowned with the rain that was falling, but licking her whiskers with the fine taste of the mouse she had caught. She squeezed through the crack just as Noah slammed the door. It caught the most of her tail and cut it clean off.

'Oh well,' said the cat, 'it was worth it!

Be bo, bend it
My tail's ended,
And I'll go to Man
    And get copper nails
And mend it.'

But she never did and that is why
Manx cats have no tails to this day.

TRADITIONAL

Letting in the Light

I am warm wrapped in my fur
My wobbly legs resting as I lie here,
My eyes still closed.
Soon they will open
Letting in the light,
And when I see
I'll spin the world round in tumbles
As I play chasing my tail,
Or hunt specks of dust in the sunlight
And wash the paws I have never seen.

My mother washes my face
Her tongue smoothing my fur,
I hear her purr,
And see, yes, some pink.
Her busy tongue, her whiskers,
Fur and eyes so orange bright,
She bends towards me,
Licking and licking,
And over I go.
I see light everywhere
      And begin to know
        I have opened my eyes.

        ELIZABETH LINDSAY

(Kittens cannot see until they are two weeks old.)

The Little White Cat

A story from France

There was once a King who had three sons. He said to them: 'I shall be lonely when I retire. Whichever of you brings me the smallest, prettiest and most intelligent little dog to keep me company, shall be King in my place.'

The three Princes set out at once. Each took a different road, agreeing to meet again in a year's time at their father's palace.

The youngest son travelled

through the world looking for the smallest and best little dog possible. One night of thunder and rain, he lost his way in a forest and came to a magnificent palace. A bell hung from the gate on a chain of diamonds, so he pulled it. The gate opened and many hands holding torches led him into the palace – yet he *saw* no one, only hands. He was led through many beautiful rooms and in the sixty-first he saw a large armchair moving by itself to a bright fire. The hands gave him clothes of silk and gold in place of his wet ones.

He was led to a lofty hall, the walls

of which were covered with paintings of cats. An orchestra of cats was playing, mewing in time and scraping the strings of the instruments with their claws.

Before the fire was a table laid for two, and a little figure in a long black veil came softly in, followed by many cats in rich court dress. To the Prince's astonishment, the black veiled figure was a beautiful little white cat! She mewed so softly and sweetly that the Prince loved her at once.

'You are welcome, Prince,' she said. 'My mewing Majesty is pleased to see you.'

'I am honoured to meet you, your Highness,' replied the Prince bowing.

The Cat and the Prince sat down, served by the hands, to a dinner of mouse pie and roast pigeon. The Prince chose the pigeon – it was delicious. He and the Cat talked together and afterwards watched a ballet of twelve cats and twelve monkeys. At night the Prince slept soundly in a room hung with tapestries of cats among butterflies of many colours.

Next day five hundred cats accompanied the Prince and the Cat Princess on a hunt. The little white Cat rode a monkey, the Prince a wooden horse which could gallop more swiftly than the wind.

Every day there was something pleasant to do and a year went by so quickly that the Prince was astonished to find that it was time to return home. How to find a dog small enough to win his father's throne?

'Prince,' purred the little Cat, 'you can ride home swiftly on the wooden horse. Here is a tiny dog more beautiful than the dog-star! Hold this acorn to your ear.' The Prince did so and heard quite plainly the bark of a tiny dog! Promising to return to his little white cat, he rode back to his father's court.

When his brothers saw him riding on a wooden horse, they said, 'What a fool he is! Where is *his* dog?' They themselves had found dainty little dogs that the King liked very well.

The Prince said nothing, but he opened the acorn and there lay the tiniest of dogs which danced so well on its hind legs that the King was charmed! However, he insisted that his sons should now find him a piece of cloth so fine that it would go through the eye of a needle.

Once more they set out. The youngest Prince rode straight back to his little white Cat. She was looking sad and thin but as soon as she saw him she sprang up in delight.

'Welcome!' she said. 'I shall always have a velvet paw for you! Stay with me and enjoy yourself. My ladies will spin you a finer cloth than your brothers can ever find.'

At the year's end a fine carriage drawn by twelve horses awaited the Prince. The Cat gave him a walnut and told him that the cloth was inside it.

'Let me stay with you,' said the Prince. 'I do not care whether I become a King or not.'

'You are kind to be fond of a little white cat!' said the Princess. 'After all, what can I do except catch mice!'

The Prince rode to his father's palace and gave him the walnut. He broke it open – inside was a hazel nut. He cracked it and there was a cherry stone. He split the kernel and inside was a millet seed. Inside *that* there was indeed a piece of cloth five hundred yards in length and so delicate that it passed through the eye of the finest needle that could be found.

Even now the King would not give up his throne. 'You must each find a beautiful maiden and I promise I will give the throne to the Prince who discovers the most beautiful of all!'

The youngest Prince hurried back to his little white Cat, who received him with soft mewings of pleasure. 'Don't worry,' she said. 'A beautiful maiden will be found for you. Meanwhile, let us be happy!'

So passed another year. 'I do not want to leave you,' said the Prince. 'Will you marry me?' He put his arms round the little white Cat – and immediately she vanished and in her place appeared a most beautiful maiden. He had released her from the wicked spell that had made her a cat.

She told him that her father had six kingdoms, but bad fairies had stolen her when she was a baby. She and all her lords and ladies were changed into cats! The only person who could rescue her was a Prince who was willing to marry a little white Cat. Now she had found one!

'Come!' said the Prince overjoyed. 'We will go at once to my father's court, for my brothers cannot possibly have found a Princess as beautiful as you!'

Together they rode to the King's court in a golden coach set with diamonds. When they were nearly there, the Princess hid herself within a sparkling crystal block veiled by silken curtains.

'Where is *your* Princess?' asked the King of his youngest son.

'I have only a little white cat,' replied the Prince. 'She mews so sweetly and has such velvet paws that you will be delighted with her.'

'What, a cat!' exclaimed the King, and the other Princes said, 'What a fool that boy is!'

The King hurried to the sparkling crystal block. It opened immediately by magic and the Princess appeared like the sun from behind clouds. Her fair golden hair was crowned with flowers and her gown was of white taffeta lined with rose silk.

'Your Highness,' she said curtseying, 'I have six kingdoms of my own. Allow me to offer one to you and one to each of your sons. Three will be enough for your youngest son and me.'

So all three Princes were married to the beautiful Princesses they had found and became Kings. They all lived happily ever after, but the youngest King and his Queen, who had once been a little white Cat, were the happiest of all.

Adapted by EILEEN COLWELL from COUNTESS D'AULNOY'S *LES FÉES À LA MODE*

Cat Nonsense

Hoddley, poddley, puddle and fogs,
Cats are to marry the poodle dogs;
Cats in blue jackets, and dogs in red
 hats;
What will become of the mice and
 rats?

ANON

My Uncle Paul of Pimlico
Has seven cats as white as snow,
Who sit at his enormous feet
And watch him, as a special treat,
Play the piano upside-down,
In his delightful dressing-gown;
The firelight leaps, the parlour glows,
And, while the music ebbs and flows,
They smile while purring the refrains,
At little thoughts that cross their brains.

                    MERVYN PEAKE

The Baker's Cat

Once there was an old lady, Mrs Jones, who lived with her cat, Mog. Mrs Jones kept a baker's shop in a little town at the bottom of a valley between two mountains.

Every morning you could see Mrs Jones's light twinkle out, long before all the other houses in the town, because she got up very early to bake loaves and buns and jam tarts and Welsh cakes. First thing in the morning Mrs Jones lit a big fire. Then she made dough out of water and sugar and flour and yeast. Then she put the dough into pans and set it in front of the fire to rise.

Mog got up early too. He got up to catch mice. When he had chased all the mice out of the bakery, he wanted to sit in front of the warm fire, but Mrs Jones wouldn't let him, because of the loaves and buns there, rising in their pans.

She said, 'Don't sit on the buns, Mog.'

The buns were rising nicely. They were getting fine and big. That is what yeast does. It makes bread and buns and cakes swell up and get bigger and bigger.

As Mog was not allowed to sit by the fire, he went to play in the sink.

Most cats hate water, but Mog didn't. He loved it. He liked to sit by the tap, hitting the drops of water with his paw as they fell, and getting water all over his whiskers.

What did Mog look like? His back, and his sides, and his legs as far as where his socks would have come to, and his face and ears and his tail were all marmalade-coloured. His stomach and his waistcoat and his paws were white. And he had a white tassel at the tip of his tail, white fringes in his ears, and white whiskers. The water made his marmalade fur go almost fox colour and his paws and waistcoat shining-white clean.

But Mrs Jones said, 'Mog, you are getting too excited. You are shaking water all over my pans of buns, just when they are getting nice and big. Run along and play outside.'

Mog was affronted. He put his ears and tail down (when cats are pleased they put their ears and tail up) and he went out. It was raining hard.

A rushing, rocky river ran through

the middle of the town. Mog went and sat in the water and looked for fish. But there were no fish in that part of the river. Mog got wetter and wetter. But he didn't care. Presently he began to sneeze.

Then Mrs Jones opened her door and called, 'Mog! I have put the buns in the oven. You can come in and sit by the fire.'

Mog was so wet that he was shiny all over, as if he had been polished. As he sat by the fire he sneezed nine times.

Mrs Jones said, 'Oh, dear, Mog, are you catching a cold?'

She dried him with a towel and gave him some warm milk with yeast in it. (Yeast is good for people when they are poorly.)

Then she left him sitting in front of the fire and began making jam tarts. When she had put the tarts in the oven she went out shopping, taking her umbrella.

But what do you think was happening to Mog?

The yeast was making him rise.

As he sat dozing in front of the fire he was growing bigger and bigger.

First he grew as big as a sheep.

Then he grew as big as a donkey.

Then he grew as big as a cart-horse.

Then he grew as big as a hippopotamus.

By now he was too big for Mrs Jones's little kitchen, but he was far too big to get through the door. He just burst the walls.

When Mrs Jones came home with her shopping-bag and her umbrella, she cried out, 'Mercy me, what is happening to my house?'

The whole house was bulging. It was swaying. Huge whiskers were poking out of the kitchen window. A marmalade-coloured tail came out of the door. A white paw came out of

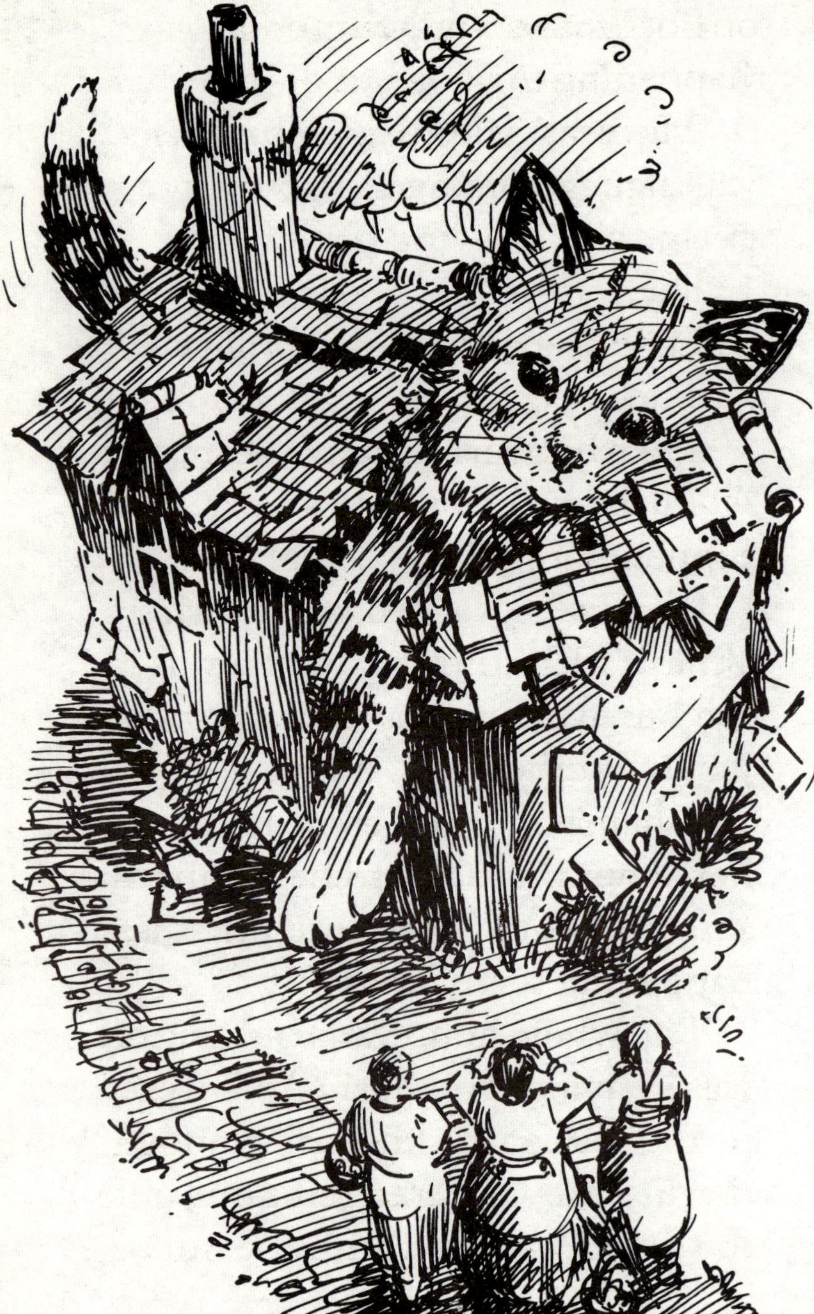

one bedroom window, and an ear with a white fringe out of the other.

'Morow?' said Mog. He was waking up from his nap and trying to stretch.

Then the whole house fell down.

'Oh, Mog!' cried Mrs Jones. 'Look what you've done.'

The people in the town were very astonished when they saw what had happened. They gave Mrs Jones the Town Hall to live in, because they were so fond of her (and her buns). But they were not sure about Mog.

The Mayor said, 'Suppose he goes on growing and growing and breaks our Town Hall? Suppose he turns fierce? It would not be safe to have him in the town, he is too big.'

Mrs Jones said, 'Mog is a gentle cat. He would not hurt anybody.'

'We will wait and see about that,' said the Mayor. 'Suppose he sat down on someone? Suppose he was hungry? He had better live outside the town, up on the mountain.'

So everybody shouted, 'Shoo! Scram! Psst! Shoo!' and poor Mog was driven outside the town. It was still raining hard. Water was rushing down the mountains. Not that Mog cared.

But poor Mrs Jones was very sad. She began making a new lot of loaves and buns in the Town Hall, crying into them so much that the dough was too wet and very salty.

Mog walked up the valley between the two mountains. By now he was bigger than an elephant – almost as big as a whale! When the sheep on the mountains saw him coming, they were scared to death and galloped away. But he took no notice of them. He was looking for fish in the river. He caught lots of fish! He was having a fine time.

By now it had been raining for so

long that Mog heard a loud watery roar at the top of the valley. He saw a huge wall of water coming towards him. The river was beginning to flood, as more and more rain-water poured down into it off the mountains.

Mog thought, 'If I don't stop that water, all those fine fish will be washed away.'

So he sat down, plump in the middle of the valley, and he spread himself out like a big, fat cottage-loaf.

The water could not get by.

The people in the town had heard the roar of the flood-water. They were very frightened. The Mayor shouted, 'Run up the mountains before the water gets to the town, or we shall be drowned.'

So they all rushed up the mountains, some on one side of the town, some on the other.

What did they see then?

Why, Mog, sitting in the middle

of the valley. Beyond him was a great lake.

'Mrs Jones,' said the Mayor, 'can you make your cat stay till we have built a dam across the valley, to keep all that water back?'

'I will try,' said Mrs Jones. 'He mostly sits still if he is tickled under his chin.'

So for three days everybody in the town took turns tickling Mog under his chin with hay-rakes. He purred and purred and purred. His purring made big waves roll right across the lake of flood-water.

All this time the best builders were making a great dam across the valley.

People brought Mog all sorts of nice things to eat, bowls of cream and condensed milk, liver and bacon, sardines, even chocolate! But he was not very hungry. He had eaten so much fish.

On the third day they finished the dam. The town was safe.

The Mayor said, 'I see now that Mog is a gentle cat. He can live in the Town Hall with you, Mrs Jones. Here is a badge for him to wear.'

The badge was on a silver chain to go round his neck. It said MOG SAVED OUR TOWN.

So Mrs Jones and Mog lived happily ever after in the Town Hall. If you should go to the little town of Carnmog you may see the policeman holding up the traffic while Mog walks through the streets on his way to catch fish in the lake for breakfast. His tail waves above the houses and his whiskers rattle against the upstairs windows. But people know he will not hurt them because he is a gentle cat.

He loves to play in the lake and

sometimes he gets so wet that he sneezes. But Mrs Jones is not going to give him any more yeast. He is quite big enough already.

JOAN AIKEN

Cats

Cats sleep
Anywhere,
Any table,
Any chair,
Top of piano,
Window-ledge,
In the middle,
On the edge,
Open drawer,
Empty shoe,
Anybody's
Lap will do,

Fitted in a
Cardboard box,
In the cupboard
With your frocks –
Anywhere!
They don't care!
Cats sleep
Anywhere.

ELEANOR FARJEON

Acknowledgements

The editor and publishers gratefully acknowledge permission to reproduce copyright material in this book:

'The Baker's Cat' by Joan Aiken from *A Necklace of Raindrops*, published by Jonathan Cape Ltd, copyright © Joan Aiken, 1968, reprinted by permission of A. M. Heath; 'The Box Under the Table' by Ruth Ainsworth from *Charles Stories and Others*, published by W. H. Heinemann Ltd, 1954, copyright © Dr F. L. Gilbert, 1954, reprinted by permission of Dr F. L. Gilbert; 'Two's Company' by Hilary Davies, reprinted by permission of the author; 'Cats' by Eleanor Farjeon from *The Children's Bells*, published by Oxford University Press, 1957, reprinted by permission of David Higham Associates; 'The Skitter-Skatter Cat' by Adrienne Jones, reprinted by permission of the author; 'Gobbolino's Hallowe'en' by Ursula Moray Williams, copyright © 1983 by Ursula Moray Williams (originally appeared in *Book of Cats* compiled by Rosemary Debnam, published by Kaye & Ward, The Windmill Press), reproduced with permission of Curtis Brown Group, London; 'Pompom and Pompinette' by Pixie O'Harris from *Cavalcade of Cats*, published by Golden Press, Sydney, 1981, copyright © The Estate of R. O. Pratt (Pixie O'Harris) c/o V. & H. Evans, reprinted by permission of The Estate of R. O. Pratt; 'My Uncle Paul from Pimlico' by Mervyn Peake from *Rhymes Without Reason*, published by Eyre and Spottiswoode, 1944, copyright © Maeve Peak, 1944, reprinted by permission of Methuen Children's Books; 'Miss Tibbles' by Ian Serraillier from *The Monster Horse*, published by Oxford University Press, 1950, copyright © Ian Serraillier, reprinted by permission of the author; 'An Unusual Basket' by Jill Tomlinson from *The Cat Who Wanted to Go Home*, published by Methuen Children's Books, 1972, copyright © The Estate of Jill Tomlinson, 1972, reprinted by permission of Methuen Children's Books; 'Kitten' from *More Small Poems* by Valerie Worth, poems copyright © 1976 by Valerie Worth, reprinted by permission of Farrar, Straus & Giroux, Inc.